Escape Velocity

THE RAGGED SKY POETRY SERIES

The Luxury of Obstacles
by Elizabeth Danson

Little Knitted Sister
by Ellen Foos

Moonmilk and Other Poems
by Carlos Hernández Peña

Between Silence and Praise
by Elizabeth Anne Socolow

Escape Velocity
by Arlene Weiner

ARLENE WEINER

Escape Velocity

RAGGED SKY PRESS

PRINCETON • NEW JERSEY

Published by Ragged Sky Press
270 Griggs Drive
Princeton, NJ 08540

Library of Congress Cataloging-in-Publication Data

Weiner, Arlene, 1941-
Escape velocity / Arlene Weiner.— 1st ed.
p. cm. — (The Ragged Sky poetry series)
ISBN-13: 978-0-9633092-9-7 (pbk.)
ISBN-10: 0-9633092-9-3 (pbk.)
I. Title. II. Series.
PS3623.E43243E83 2006
811'.6—dc22 2005030240

Some of the poems in this book originally appeared in the following publications: *The Louisville Review; Pleiades, a Journal of New Writing; Poet Lore; U.S. 1 Newsweekly; U.S. 1 Worksheets.*

This book is composed in Gotham and Minion

Text and cover design by Foos Rowntree
Cover art: detail of *E#2*, 2004, oil on canvas, 30"x24" by Jean Foos

Manufactured in the United States of America

First Edition

A R L E N E W E I N E R has worked as a college instructor, a cardiology technician, a research associate with a group developing educational software, and an editor. She grew up in Inwood, near the northern tip of Manhattan, and has lived in Massachusetts, California, Pittsburgh, and Princeton, New Jersey.

Contents

ESCAPE VELOCITY

THESE FIGS

Acknowledgments

Many, many thanks to those who have encouraged me in writing poetry, and especially to Gerry Sandson, Michael Wurster, and the members of Pittsburgh Poetry Exchange and U.S. 1 Poets' Cooperative. To Ellen Foos, whose friendship and skill made this book a practical reality. To Elizabeth Socolow, for brilliant readings, warm hospitality, and many other helps. To my mother, who introduced me to poetry. To Ted, Barbara, Doug, Em, Gillian, and Shas. And to my husband, who has proposed that I spend my mornings writing and my afternoons drinking coffee from a saucer in a coffee shop.
It may yet happen!

The A Train

expressed. It is a song
smiling mouth.

power of

Close Reading

I'm going to   read you.

I'm going to   eye you in the store
I'm going to   pick you up
I'm going to   take you home
I'm going to   flex your spine
I'm going to open   your uncut pages
I'm going to run my fingers   along your lines.

Yes, I'm going to move my lips.
Yes, I'm going to say every sound   out loud.
Yes, I'm going to get my tongue   around
every part of you.

And then
I'm going to   do it some more
till I get down
till I get down to your core.

Till you cry out to me.

I'm going to read you
I'm going to read you
like you've never been read before.

Cirque de Lune

—for Michael Wurster

You take me to a circus in the dark,
buy me candy and a fake
snake. I'm a child.

I hear the slap of blind
trapeze artists making catches.
An odor of elephant then
or drunk men waltzing in leather.

When they announce the knife thrower
and his beautiful wife
I feel something slide
quick quick cold cold against my side.

Best of all, the calliope.
Faint, grateful. I hold my breath,
it stops.

At the last,
for the recessional,
a clown plays guitar in Spanish

and one white light, high,
round, pale, comes on
and the audience
is illuminated.

The A Train

Waiting on the platform
for the train to Brooklyn, back
in the subway and on my own,
when on the opposite track
the A comes in.

If I crossed over I'd
catch it uptown, slide
past Billy Strayhorn's stop,
wouldn't drop off in Harlem, I'd ride
all the way to Dyckman.

And find what? Not
the second-run movie house
where I saw Brando play
Napoleon in *Desirée*
and white culottes,
memorably.

If I did it right, I'd change
at the deepest station, 168th—
black kids at the end of the tube
braiding voices for their own echoes—
catch the IRT

to Inwood, the train leaning rickety
round the curve into air,
go down the iron stair
to the station below,
where the stove's mica window would glow,

pass dust-colored birds in the street,
find the woman in the little store
who'd sell me one piece of marzipan,
fuzzy on the tongue
and too sweet.

The Magician

A carnival near the Speedway
when reeds grew green.
Nobody so green then
as a New York girl.

My father shimmered.
Mother stayed to learn
the earliest illusion
the cup and ball.

He put me like a red scarf
up her sleeve.
For years I watched her washing out
his high hat's silk.

The feathers and blood.

A Craft

—for my mother

Vermeer's lacemaker's hands,
as she bends to her bobbin,
are blessed by a milky light,

but your knuckles dance,
complicating a string,
in mere air, mirrored

in windows of permanent night.
The subway roars and screeches.
Turned toward somebody's talk,

your face takes no notice
as your fingers row
autonomous, knotting a net.

A hook rocks in your right hand,
catches a twist from the left, and grows
an endless coil, a snail,

saucer, bowl, almost a globe.
And caught in it will flash
sequins like dimes, silver night-fish.

You are making a hat for Othello's head
or Crystal's. It will cradle the skull.
Your web will keep them warm

in a New York winter.
The knack of this, the skill.
Simple. The keeping at it.

Money Then

was palpable and familiar
as the geranium in the barber's window;
like the leaves of a silver maple:
one side gray-green, one green-gray.

It wrinkled into softness, like great-
grandmother's cheek. New,
it was crisp in banded stacks
as ironed shirts.

I saw a man count a deck of it,
holding it up to his ear
while he riffled the edges
with his thumb.

Fathers said, *Do you think*
money grows on trees?
although in my neighborhood
there were no trees.

Soon only children and the poor
will know the feel of it, snap.
Weight of coins,
their bitter taste.

1959

Is it hot enough for you?
the neighbor said on the stairs
to the girl in gloves. *Hot enough*
for you? said the subway conductor,
closing the doors. *Hot*
enough? the elevator man
to the girl in a shirtwaist dress,
one of many white girls,
in summer gloves, hair damp
on her neck, on her way
to the typing pool. She laughed
for the colored man moving
the brass control through its arc.

In the big room where the men
yelled into phones at debtors
fans turned. Ribbons fluttered
on the round cages to indicate breezes.
In the center of the room
an iron mesh, floor to ceiling,
surrounded the typists. Little jackets
hung on the backs of their chairs.

After work, elevator, subway,
stairs, supper. Maybe a movie,
Twenty degrees cooler inside.
Maybe an Esther Williams.

They never said, *Fast enough*
for you? Deep enough? High enough?
They never said then, *Far enough?*
Far enough for any of us?

Before TV

When there was nothing else to look at
the sky was big screen

There were just two channels
dark and light

We watched interference
thinking it was a program

We thought the remote was up there
changing us

Cancellations

For Nancy

I bought limes, Nancy,
thinking there would be time
for gin and tonic on my porch.
I know there will be no new Edward Goreys
and that every breath you took was an effort
but there will be *Atlantic* puzzles
and pleasurable murders,
cozies even; there are still
stray cats, stray people
to round up on Christmas Eve
to drink your creamy eggnog
around the little skaters on the mirror lake
with the fake snow, the real warmth,
in your rooms packed with books
and quirky beautiful objects
(although the cats edited them severely,
sweeping your crystal ornaments off the table),
and I know you felt pain in your bones,
and I'm not angry, not really,
although you should have given me time
to write a poem you could hear
and time to squeeze limes for you
and time to hear again your voice like cream;
and you so clever shouldn't have let
the most likely suspect do you in,
the idiot who fills in the puzzle
at random, sweeps away
the sturdy and the delicate,
breaks flesh and bones,
takes the breath away—
shouldn't have let him
orphan the little skaters,
leave the cats twice orphaned,
and all of us, all of us here
remembering you.

Elegy for a Pug

She's gone, your squat prancer,
who was ridiculous and delicate.
No one who saw you with her could imagine
your love depends on money, looks, or wit.

Her mug was uglier than an August bug's.
She was dumb, but answered
your words, speaking in her own fashion.
She was naked, but gave rich gifts.

And you, fastidious, gave her permission
to paw and tongue you, to snuffle in shit,
to eat flesh raw, because your ugly angel
was of a warmer, earlier creation.

Life List

All those sightings, pursuits, bad weather,
climbs, disappointments, epitomized.
The blue kingfisher true to the crooked stream.
Cardinal at the sill, common but she hopes
heartlifting. Exotic dream in the desert,
scissor-tailed flycatcher.
Duck, dickcissel, indeterminate brown sparrow
elusive in the scrub. This life list,
reticent, small-sized,
ordered and numbered. His life
contracted into a fist.
If we pried it might hide
only two pennies,
or a found robin's-egg shell, an owl's
barbless down feather.

City Morning

I’ve passed the men holding out empty cups
and passed the fair young couple, unshaped as slugs,
humped under plastic on the library steps.

I’ve seen the ornery man put off a bus,
and nightsticked into a wagon by a cop,
and muttering along the sidewalk with his legs
in the starred pajamas of the mental ward.

I’ve nodded to the blond man with the beard
leading his dogs, one with a blind blue eye,
up from under the bridge into the day.

But this is hard: on a table in the park
a man asleep. Around him, merchandise.
His forty balloons in party colors bob,
sticks threaded providently through the cracks.

To Our Father

Where is your ram now? The hand lifts the blade,
the fire leaps gloating for the flesh
in Jerusalem, in Ramallah, in Rwanda, in Sri Lanka.
The thicket is empty. The sacrifice is made.

Where is your fountain? We thirst in the desert.
Our mother turns so she won't see us die
in Somalia, in Australia, in Brooklyn, on the North Side.
Our father is absent. The watersack is dry.

Who lifts up the needy, who gives grain and corn?
Who parts the angry waters so we pass unmolested?
In a garage in Homewood, on a street in Inwood,
we look for our defender. Our flesh is torn.

Our fists struck our hearts as we confessed:
we were arrogant, we were brutal, we condoned wrongdoing...
All of us did thus. We are made in your likeness.
Turn to us. Your stone heart beats in our chest.

Fall Color

I am thinking of my father's slow fall
as I walk past Marc's house, his sluggish heart,
his wine-colored legs, and my mother's call
to say he's spitting up blood. In Marc's yard
his two trees have begun to turn,
one before the other. They burn
salmon against a perfect sky.
Beautiful. I must call my mother, fly
or drive to New York. It's still warm, most trees
are holding their leaves, green,
except those stressed by drought or disease.
Soon all of them will learn
what Marc's trees know. But I put by
that knowledge for winter, and enjoy
their unusual flame for this time.
I think of calling Marc, to say, in March
take your son out in the cold, tap
the stripped trees, let him put out his tongue
for the slow run of sweet sap.

—Pittsburgh, October 2001

What the Night Nurse Said

When she woke up
we dressed it like a daughter
and brought it to her
and propped it so she could see.

For Jesus' sake! she said
Where is the face?
The front of the head
was pink as this palm
smooth as a footsole.

It curved in like a bean
and had two creases running right across
but that was all
nothing you could call features.

Such poor creatures
never live long
she whispered to her pillow.
When she turned back
we held it out to her.
She looked again. *At least*

it can't be suffering
she said. That was when
the upper crease
let down two drops of water.

Cancellation

Dear Sir or Madam:
I seem inadvertently to have signed up
or been signed up for the Death of the Month Club
and the deaths have been coming so frequently
that I haven't had time to say, Stop.
I now have more than enough deaths
to last my lifetime and can give scant attention
even to the important deaths that everyone's talking about,
the deaths long-awaited or overnight sensations,
precocious deaths. In the past
when the rubber tree relinquished its leaves
one by one, or a friend's dog died,
I gave them serious consideration,
but I was young then, warm enough, and had hammock time
for melancholy wisdom. So dear, dear Sir,
merciful Madam, I hope you will agree
to stop my subscription, and if I have accrued
any bonus points, and you allow substitutes,
please send me instead preserves and tropical fruits.

A Little Spanish Song

My friend calls me over to see his pet.
I've captured a cricket—
You know they bring luck!
He is so happy that I can't tell him
he's cradling a cockroach in his pocket.

Ay, ay, ay—Love never gets tired
of playing the same miracle over and over.

My friend holds his pet up to his ear.
Ah, she is singing, don't you hear it?
All I hear is his breathing
and the cockroach chewing.
It's music to him.

Ay, ay, ay—Love never gets tired
of playing the same miracle over and over.

My friend plays guitar, there's music in his house
and what does it matter if he's trying to follow
the voracious rasping of a roach?
Why can't I sing along, why can't I swallow
the bread I am given at my friend's table?

Ay, ay—stupid Love just never gets tired
of playing the same miracle over and over.

"While You Were Out"

Bad news, boychik—the girlfriend just checked
if you'd be in town. That was no chat—that chick
doesn't waste time, doesn't miss a trick.
With your back turned now I know you can expect
the goldplated shaft. She'll borrow your car
or maybe your flat. You may find it wrecked
or maybe just used. Or you'll never suspect.

Things aren't what they were. Things are what they are.
I feel such a loser. I feel so bruised.
Well, we lived and laughed. And how. We cruised
with the top put down when it was warm,
all around town. Now, back to the form:
While you were out Lindsey *called. The time. The date.*
I'll check *Left no message. Will call back.*—Kate.

Outplacement

When they calculate the grease
is running low
and they put you out on a floe
with a purse of dried codfish and an oar,

do not by any means row for the shore
paddling to decrease
the black water between you,
or watch in hope that a leopard seal,

attracted to their store, consume them.
Build a small fire, make fishhooks,
raise your one sealskin as a sail.
Fix on the horizon. Keep warm. Move on.

Half House

[illegible] twenty horse-
[illegible] course they will
[illegible] they must be.

Tropical Wedding

—after Claude Levi-Strauss

The Bororo say: a woman wed a tapir.
He could show her the wide world.
He bedded her in the forest, grunting
and rooting. It was wonderful.
She visited her family
at Thanksgiving—he'd gone hunting
to be sure of getting his deer.
When they saw their girl covered with ticks
her mother tried to pull off a fat one.
Daughter turned away. *That*
is one of my husband's pearls.

Xanadu to Zugzwang

I'm studying the Encyclopedia
of Love. I've already worked through
Volume 1: *Abasement to Boudoir*
and Volume 2: *Bower to Desperation.*
I found *Destiny to Dysfunction,*
Eagerness to Fiasco, Hesitant to Hot
but I see there are gaps. I think
you've been studying, too. By now
you must know by heart *How to Hurt.*

A Couple at an Exhibition of Hopper Paintings

They know these scenes. These clamant silences.
The honey trapezoids on the blue walls.
The windows, beds, and parapets that are walls
beyond which some sort of life
seems to occur.

They know the bending grass,
the vixen dog prepared to bound,
the harridan shouting to an afternoon
that is solid and deaf.
The golden, round,
and shining fruit that is nearly in reach.

The eye yearns for the fragrance of the fruit.
The parched eye crosses into
the hot dark wood.
The eye strains to hear what the grass says
to the unseen sea.

Always a bedhead, parapet, road.
Uncrossable.
The framed night window. The grassy space.

Yet sometimes
a woman leans toward you,
thinking of something else,
her white arm reaching, placing the fruit
or casually draped on the table,
and sometimes her arm seems to you

a white bridge breaking the glass of the afternoon,
promising fragrance.
Frail bridge! It is never enough, never able
to bear your whole weight over into the music.

I look at you out of the frame
of the black doorway,
my red mouth sipping
its first smoke of the day.

Fatalities

Waiting for him and he a little late,
the children grown, the supper on the stove,
there's a pause she is glad of, leisure
for a minor section of the morning paper,

Of Regional Interest. She reads. On the pike
an accident. In daylight and dry weather
a truck eastbound, a semi, has turned over,
and toppling across the barrier, crushed a car

opposing. The driver killed outright
and a passenger, a father and mother.
Their son pried out, flown to a trauma unit.
The trucker walked away, injuries minor,

no alcohol, no drugs in him. "Appearing stunned"
he told how his load shifted on a bend.
He, feeling it behind him, tried to swerve
but tipped. And so two, maybe three, were dead.

Solitary, struck, she thinks of her husband,
wanting to share it, make him marvel at it.
A marvel can be a marvel though evil.
A family picked out, as a spot on the sea

is picked out at random by a beam
of sun among clouds. And if a bird
in the spot is illuminated, still random.
The road turned, the load

shifted. It was nobody's fault.
But he would argue, would cite laws
that existed or ought to exist, probable cause,
the road's engineering, the truck

probably for profit overloaded
the driver undertrained or overtired…
anything but her truth—that there's no blame
and no consolation, which (she sees)

is saying much the same. The load shifts.
A family is extinguished or not. No one's at fault.
Now his approaching high-beams touch the paper
and she puts it down on the table and rises to greet him.

What Onions Want

What do onions want, I wonder.
What do they need?
Maples want so to breed
that the lawn is full of their seed.

Onions do not seduce.
Why, then, such juice?
Why the sweetness that comes
after slow heat?

They are neither bubble nor stone
but want neither mother nor wife.
They want to keep their skins whole,
to be let alone.

Blind, I put down the knife.

The Maladroit

Is always there with a knife when you need a spoon.
Is always there with a basket instead of a pail.
Is always there like a star when you want a moon.
When you crave applause is folding her hands in prayer.

A knife may serve for eating the fragrant melon.
A basket dipped in the water swells and holds.
Unruffled, the lake on a clear night reflects a star.
Prayer can be sung, or the kind ear hear it as song.

But what can be done with the heart, the offered heart,
the maladroit, unwanted, idiot heart,
the panhandling slut on the street, with her lips in your face
closing and opening their vulgar red
unstoppable unforgivable "Bub, Bub, Bub"?

A Ray

Two on a beach lay together.
Unspeaking one arose
and swam out far, as if dared.
Slowly rose the other
to take the first in care.
About them the blue weather
smiled, and lied.

He swam, growing less and less.
She watched with harpoon stare:
turn or sink she thought.
She beat her wings a while
but if he had been caught
in the fist of an evil tide
she found she could not aid.
And she was glad.

Then from a further wave
a dark angel reared:
horned, splendid,
a light-annihilating kite.
On leather wings wide-extended,
it stilled for minutes or seconds
and disappeared.

And whether it sprang or sank,
whether it barred or beckoned,
she exulted, she did not fear.

A Garden in Pittsburgh

This madcap, made-much-of, little garden
for a half house is higgledy-piggle
with cabbages, statuary, rosebushes
high as my head and spectacularly red
in October with fruits, not flowers.
I giggle at its pride: lions the size
of Lhasa Apsos that challenge
the central path, there being I suppose
not enough room for front-facing guardians.
Whatever knife cleft the house—history,
law, or private wrath?—left a roof sloping
only one way, though no neighbor abuts,
only sky. And here and now, in Lawrenceville,
where the blank back of the Teamsters' Temple
and Radiant Hall's dull front disappoint,
where Home Street runs down to the avenue
of exhausted warehouses, I vow
if ever I live in a half house I'll defy
the knife, plant yuccas and artichokes,
pinwheels and pennants, fill a dry fountain
with zinnias, erect a Venus
with a ventral clock, seed clouds
with flowering cabbages, live
a whole life under the doubled sky.

Escape Velocity

Lamentation

By the great river that flows two ways
I met him. Then I was a yellow boat
for the wreathed king. During the longest days
in that flat country we rowed
among reed birds to the border of the sea.

At the border of the sea, painted with sun, I thirsted.
We drank each other at the river mouth.
Salt, fresh. He was whole then, his thighs
a branched tree. Now I burst
with salt pain like a shad in spring.

Winter after winter he has lain with my rival.
He has wreathed his head with her heavy gray crown.
She has clasped him between her icy thighs, and strewn
his members along the rivers. Shad, where did you travel?
Bitterns, where were you? Why did you not cry out?

Spring after spring along the rivers
I have searched for his scattered parts,
gathered them, stitched them together
with song. I have sung with a drying throat.
This spring, this spring, I cannot find his heart.

I will cry out for the long days, the sun,
the green wreath. I will swim to the fresh water,
deliver myself of salt. Oh, my black opponent,
will you give me your lead shoes, will I lie down with you,
can I love you, since you have won, my beautiful one?

So Be It

I wanted to walk with you, speak plainly,
listen quietly, possibly take your hand.
But my spaniel began wagging its tail insanely,
my retriever was bounding away and back and away,
and you couldn't come out without your baby
who's quiet in general, winning sometimes,
but just now is inconsolable and a handful.
And my dogs bound so, circle me, claim attention.

Just now one is pleading for me
to throw a stick, and I throw
and she brings back a simile, and invention
starts inventing while discovery
slips away, not like your cat shyly
but like the wild rainbow, swimming so strongly
that it stays still, while I on a raft shoot by unaware
on my mettle for rapids and will not stay

and the moment is of no moment
and the good talk has died.
So I will walk out with my dogs
and you'll care for your child
and you'll go one way and I'll go another way.

Lightening

Straining, in pain,
on a tilting deck
I've dragged sacks of salt
over the rail, back to the sea.

Blood, tears, the secret humors of the body
are salt, we are continent,
our ocean interior.
Its tide hammers in the throat.

I thought I was a buoyant, tall ship,
I could carry a lading of salt,
lemons, wine, and fripperies
Not Wanted on the Voyage.

The world's awash, the sky dark.
Swamped in the sea, I look
for a plank, bobbing cask, tea chest,
to carry me from the wrack.

Ashore, if I get to shore, if I find
dry land, sweet water, light,
I may forget, renew appetite
for scented baths, rocking chairs, salt for food.

Escape Velocity

I'm going
round and around you
or you're going
round and around me.
Or more correctly we
are a system bound
to go round and around and around
in our accustomed places.

So we're going
a headlong breakneck pace
in stasis.
Round and around like waltzing
sweating white Lipizzaner horses
and barring some jolt or bolt
we'll keep going
round and around and around
in our courses.
It's as easy as falling…
it *is* falling.

Escape velocity is the energy to change.
To stand still and be left behind.
It is the immense amount
of energy it takes to stay
at rest
and let the rest
fall
away.

Dying Is Easy

Dying is easy—*comedy* is hard.
—*Theater proverb*

If algebra is easy, poetry
is hard; if driving is easy,
riding is hard. If walking
is easy, parking is hard.
Health, pleasure, leisure:
easy. Money hard.
Listening easy? thinking hard.
Disease isn't easy, ease
isn't always easy.
If dying is easy, mourning's hard.
And if loving is easy, leaving's
hard, hard, hard, hard, hard.

Exit Wound

—after H. Damasio et al., "The Return of Phineas Gage..."
Science, *20 May 1994*

There once was a man who was sober and industrious,
who paid his bills and kept his word.
He worked tamping powder on the Burlington and Rutland.
One day an unfortunate accident occurred.

An iron spike went clean through his skull.
Of course he was ill. But he recovered.
This red line through the orbit and passing through the cranium
shows the zone affected and the exit inferred.

This happened long ago, in another age,
so you see his survival was doubly a miracle.
After that the unfortunate Phineas Gage
went from job to job—they were mostly menial—
and couldn't keep them. He was given to rage
and became unreliable.

He went to South America and worked as a drover.
His respect for the conventions having disappeared
he was said to have become a lubricious lover.
At least that's what the villagers heard.

This interesting incident is evidence
that the frontal region is the locus
of our moral sense.
Had he been damaged at another focus

he might have been a drooling wreck
but his probity, we expect,
would have been intact. He would have retained
the gratitude and modesty that had previously marked him.

Of course one can't experiment now
unless you examine those who begin
modest, grateful, and reliable, yet somehow
in maturity begin to caper and grin—

who clap hands and sing, or take many lovers
or in public places fall to their knees.
Doubtless they have some internal lesion,
some corrupting disease, tumor or the like
in the frontal region.

Some red shaft or spike.

These Figs

With Care

I'm wrapping your birthday present,
a photograph of Charles Mingus,
moody and smoke-veiled, with his bass,
and I'm feeling incompetent,
as if I'd like help, and as always
when I feel incompetent, as if someone
would help, but who? your father
so competent at wrapping, isn't here,
your brother recently told me, *Don't*
fetishize your incompetence, and you
are across the continent, maybe across the planet,
as good as across the universe. The photograph
of Charles Mingus is protected with glass
so I have to protect the glass,
and I'm using a breadknife
to saw styrofoam packing saved
in case we ever had to return the object
that came in it, which I realize,
since it was an electric typewriter,
I'll never have to return, or want to return,
and may have discarded already.
I've wrapped Charles Mingus
in the softer foam that protected
the elegant circular perpetual calendar
that you gave me for my birthday,
although I've reached the age when I know
that I don't need a perpetual calendar,
because time doesn't move in a circle,
and I'm beginning to think, Isn't this good enough,
if I mark it *Fragile?* isn't the purpose
of marking it *Fragile* to see
that care will be taken?
and hasn't Charles Mingus had enough bad luck
already, to deserve in the afterlife

to walk through the fire unscathed
or at least through the terrible machines
of the postal system?
but I know that care isn't always taken
with the fragile and deserving
and if Charles Mingus arrives damaged,
or if you already have a photograph
of Charles Mingus, or if a photograph
of Charles Mingus is a nuisance
because you'll have to move it
on your next and imminent move,
please understand that the moody,
veiled, but deep bass rhythm
of my life and of your life
says I love you and carry you still.

A Gift of Soap

The soap on my skin
this morning told me *Practice*
love. Love the legs
with their veins and scars, love
the cracked feet, the freckled
hands. The soap said *touch*
the skin, *linger*
over the tender places—
that palms and fingers
see better than eyes.
Take comfort. Care
for the damaged and whole,
the scarred and smooth.
Take your wrinkled life, learn
how to make a husband
of your hands.

The soap is heavy and good,
I know it will last.

Good Shoes

The shoes are tired of waiting.
They went to two weddings
and the first night of a play
but for a long time they have stood empty.

They are too good
to stand in the rain, too stiff
to stride in the street.
They are a little out of fashion.

They think of going out by themselves.
Of clicking down corridors,
down steps. Of being kicked off
in a hotel chamber.

Of standing next to sandals
at the doorway of a ryokan,
leaving their impressions
on a page of fresh snow,

meeting other shoes,
whirling and stamping,
going to Barcelona
to dance the intricate sardana,
circling laid-aside parcels
and purses in the plaza.

Privet Flower

In a neglected neighborhood
where tree roots heave up sidewalks
and mulberries stain cars
I stand on a June evening
and drink a delicious scent.

Not rose or magnolia
who open their hearts all day
but the pale unnoticed daughter
who lights her lamp
in the burgher's hedge
or the tree of the ignorant man
the lilac's small sister
casts this song on the night.

The privet who casts her scent
across the sidewalk
distracts me from my business
or recalls me.

Hawk Mountain

On a bone in the spine
of a sleeper
whose head's in Maine
tailbone in Georgia
a crow's nest of a flagship
on a tree-green sea
stone lens focusing warmth
where hawks are drawn
in their long float south
toward warmer nights
we gather to see these fliers.

Girl Scouts crunch apples
student nurses chat
a den of panting Cubs
unships their packs.
Two Auduboners talk binoculars
while experts radio to outliers
two sharpshins northwest
'shoulder coming up
three 'tails over the valley

and one beaky crone
old as the hills
northfacing
lets her wrists float up
broadwinged
her fingers spreading
in the autumn sun
and knowing
rocks in quiet
on the height.

A Yard in New Jersey

I eat cantaloupe in the yard
of a rented house. Clay
that refused rain has drained, hardens
into brick. Once a gardener,
among tufts of coarse grass
and strawberry leaves
I've turned only a tiny plot
for red salvia, inviting hummingbirds.

Against the house wall three daylilies
hold themselves above rampant mint,
the work of a past tenant.
I cut back the bridal-veil
to give them light. They'll live.
In second-growth woods daylilies
ring abandoned housepits
as mushroom necklaces in grass
trace oaks long gone.

I scoop and scrape the melon flesh, color
of daylilies, leaving a thin canoe, greenish,
from which I drink the liquor. Greedy, I can't
get enough of the good-enough,
packaged strawberries, hard green apples,
birdsong in the yard, nights with somebody.
The flowers are not tiger lilies. Tomorrow
they will be shriveled gloves on their stalks.

I take the rind to cast on the pile
that's my mark on the land, my midden
taking in rind, husk, core, stem, grounds,
unwanted, wilted, rotten, sprouted-unbidden,
and cover it with ungloved hands.
Here the green canoe is not hidden, not stored,
but gone to glory, and I the nourisher
of the heap, turning it, churning the life after life.

Solstice

I've set out the two-armed sprinkler
and turned up the water
and a robin has come like an heir
to the new-moistened ground.

It isn't the rain of nature,
that thrums and ripples
with summer lightning.
Still he probes the moist ground

as I sit and watch the water dancing,
the great sleeves' gesture
describing the pull of earth on water,
driving itself, playing the play

of what is and will be, what goes on
whether our gardens bloom
or rot or wither,

the play that will continue
when we are gone
with our air and our earth and our water.

And it's evening.
The robin is stationing himself on a wire
to sing the day to dark.

Soon I will stretch my two arms to the night
as fireflies enter, their cool torches
glowing like upward meteors, to prolong
long long this longest of the days.

February Thaw

Homing on narrow roads between starved farms
I start at deer that stare into my light
as I into their dark. It's Valentine's night.
Cold rain comes down as if it meant me harm.

A snow shovel's propped at my door, a charm
against more snow. Rain sluiced away the bright
twin of the house that lay against it, like a white
shadow, this morning. Now I feel I can't get warm.

You're in a far city, where my storms
don't trouble you—nor do you share my flights.
We meet to celebrate, observe forms,
even enjoy occasional delight.
Cold rain comes down as if it meant me harm.
More and more I miss the heat of your arms.

Amaryllis

Most of the year you're no beauty—
a squat lump in the dirt
then for a long time comical,
a pair of green bunny ears.

I don't know why I keep you going.
A kind of pride—in what? all you require
is neglect, and then care
of the most minimal sort,

just to be set upright and given water.
Actually it's attention I give—
moving the pot around, touching
the soil with my fingertips, watching

a long, long time for green, and despairing
that nothing will come this year,
no leaves spring. And here in February
all there is to see

is a blunt arrow hardly distinguishable
from a leaf, unpromising flat bud,
showing, this Valentine's Day,
only a faint reddening.

We've come a long way together
my vegetable love,
and I watch not only for the miraculous
rather vulgar coral flower

that you'll shake out of your sleeve
nor for your wand's green thrust
but for your earliest unfisting
after the autumn thirst.

Old Moon,

you used to be

my ripe melon, love's food,
low in the sky.

Now you're up high,
a thin dime.

Still you come up heads for me
every time.

Autograph Party

After she misspent her youth,
sent her children away, betrayed
her country, burned her chairs,
table, house, to feed her fire,
broke off being a wife and shamed
her lovers, caused her mother
to be spat upon in the public square,
after she learned to tell, not the truth,
but a truth and another truth and another,
upraising the dark lamp of early harm
that calls out shadows in others,

she's earned a name and the right
to read before this small audience
of the callow and the balding,
the uncomprehending, the appalled,
leaning heavily first on the chairman's arm,
then on the lectern. Then some come up praising
her earliest work, that she likes least,
and curious about the life, and saying
they think they'd like to do the same,
always meant to. Mean to, someday.

These Figs

This tray of figs in the market
fresh and round, touched green.
I weigh two in the hollows of my hands.
The pressed mahogany sweets
my mother took to mourners' houses
didn't presage soft figs and yellow lemons
as in a California garden by the sea
where I carried a child.
I missed harsh seasons there,
though the great wheel daily turned
through warmth and chill.

A friend sends a postcard picturing
"Santa Barbara's magnificent Moreton Bay fig."
Thirty years ago in the dazzle of possibilities
I didn't see that broad hundred-year-old god.
Once though, at a coastal warfare lab,
I saw with joy a spreading fig,
a broad Moreton fig, and dolphins at play.
The rooted tree let flourish for its beauty—
the dolphins, I later learned, were harnessed weapons.

~

The morning paper says dolphins kill.
Their intense play may mean rescue or assault.
Yet it is play.
And for play
and for the tree, the fruit,
for the shade, the sun,
for the dazzle of shade with sun
for the form of the tree

for the upright tree
for the spreading tree

for the form of the leaf
the small leaf
the great
the leaf like a lance
the leaf like a violin
the pore
the petiole
for the movement of air in the leaves
for the trunk with its milk
for the trunk that has no milk
for the changing from leafless to leafed
and from leafed to leafless
and for the unchanging
I when they come to me
will pause in joy

And when it comes to me
for the sleek body tearing the water
for the seamless water
for the play of the water on the body
and the play of the body
in the water

And for the eating
and for the eaten
will pause in joy

Will pause in joy for these, these figs
these present figs
soft and ripe.

Lightning Source UK Ltd.
Milton Keynes UK
UKOW02f0000220316

270629UK00001B/3/P

9 780963 309297